FATHERLESS SONS
THE CRY OF OUR FATHERLESS GENERATION

BY DEMETRIUS ZEIGLER

I'mMyOwnMan

Fatherless Sons
The Cry of Our Fatherless Generation
All Rights Reserved.
Copyright © 2014 Demetrius Zeigler
v1.0

Front Cover Design © 2014 Tim Demit. All rights reserved - used with permission.

ISBN: 978-0-578-14053-7

PRINTED IN THE UNITED STATES OF AMERICA

*"I cannot think of any need in childhood
as strong as the need for a father's protection"*

-Sigmund Freud

Contents

Introduction...i

Part One: Parenthood
The Traits of a Father 1
The Role of a Father..5
What Being a Father Means to Me 7
Words from Mom 11
Words from another Mom 13

Part Two: The Boys' Stories
My Story Living in an Abusive Household 21
My Teen Years 33
Challenging Yourself...37
In Retrospect..45
God, I'm Letting It Go 49
Daniel's Story 51

Robert's Story..69

David's Story..73

John's Story..77

Jason's Story...89

Part Three: The Products of Fatherless Homes

Statistics of Fatherless Sons......................................97

Famous People Who Grew up Without Fathers.....101

Conclusion

Power of Forgiveness 109

Afterword...113

Introduction

Youth in today's society have been faced with an epidemic that sometimes can alter the way in which a child grows up. This epidemic can change the way young men and women view the world we live in today. Many fatherless sons and daughters are abandoned by father figures and left with a struggling home, a broken heart, and the lack of trust. Fatherless Sons like me have to take responsibility at a very young age due to the absence of our fathers. Some of us are faced with the headaches of living in a single-parent home, or in my house a fatherless home.

In our generation, we have to agree that fathers who have abandoned their children are considered deadbeat dads. Men and women alike do not connect with or trust this type of men. A very big percentage of women would say that fathers who have abandoned their children are cowards, punks, and losers.

But what do we call fathers that are absent from a child's life not by choice? What do we call fathers that are incarcerated, or suffer from their own insecurities? Can we label fathers as deadbeat dads if their own fathers were absent from their lives? Can we label fathers as deadbeat dads, knowing that the lack of father figures left them lonely and afraid? The purpose of this book, Fatherless Sons, is to share the different lives of fatherless sons from young men's, single mothers', and fathers' perspectives.

Part One
Parenthood

The Traits of a Father

Today I would say that not all fathers absent from homes are deadbeat dads. Some are strong men who are facing their own dilemmas. Some are afraid to admit that they failed raising their children, and others may be afraid to return home.

We have to agree that the role of a father plays a very unique part in a child's life. Having a father can determine a lot in the way that a child grows up and what he or she becomes in his or her life. Being a father isn't always going be easy; there are always many challenges that will be faced in the years that a child becomes an adult. I must say that some of the best people in the world grow up with single parents and have to learn how to be responsible at an early age.

There is good and bad in every situation, and not having a father isn't the worst thing in the world; but I must admit that a father does play a very essential role in a child's life. In our generation, it's not very common to see a father in every home that you may enter. I can say that many of us are struggling now due to the fact that we didn't have fathers there to teach us how to be strong and pick ourselves back up when we were knocked down. But that can change; and it's time to start something new and set a new bar for the generations that will come after us.

What is the role of a father? First, he is to be responsible, to do right by his wife as well as his child. This means being a good husband. He must love, honor, nourish and cherish his wife in every aspect of her life; only then will he be prepared to be a good father.

The second needed trait of a father is accountability; a man must hold full accountability for his words, thoughts, and actions towards his family. And the third is possibility; as a father, he must make it possible for his children to grow up in a positive light, to want to be something better than the rapper on the TV, and to make it possible to lead his children in a spiritual path so that they may live in a spiritual home, and progress into living for themselves in a spiritual life. These are the most important roles of a father, the goals of fatherhood, and generally what being a father is really all about.

Christopher Ruff, 2013

The Role of a Father

Like many, I am a fatherless child. I grew up knowing my father's name, but not knowing who the man was behind the name. The word "father" speaks volumes to me, knowing I am going to be a father soon. I have resentment toward my father for the fact that he acknowledges my sisters, but looks past me.

I grew up curious and angry, trying to figure out if it was something I had done or said, trying to figure out why I was abandoned, why I was thrown to the side, just forgotten about. I have rarely discussed this with anyone, but I was angry for years. I found myself punching walls, acting out, but for the most part, I kept a lot of the anger bottled up. I could feel myself going the wrong way, not caring for school or life, but I met someone and accepted them into my life. I started to pray, and worship, and love.

I found a new beginning. I had to learn to forgive my father. Now I look at the word "father" and it means so much. A father is an enforcer, a lover, an idol, a role model, a protector, a leader. A father is the head of the house, the provider, the one you run to when you need help. Now don't get me wrong, a mother is important, but a father has qualities that a mother doesn't have. A father is the one who instills certain qualities in a child.

Father" is one word that has a million meanings. I was without a father, but I know in my heart and mind that when my child gets here and someone asks him/her, "What does the word 'father' mean?" He/she will be able to answer that question with his/her head high and mind flowing. Because, I'll be the father that I would have wanted to grow up with and learn from. I know that for a fact. **I'm My Own Man**

-James Wilson

What Being a Father Means to Me

Becoming a father changed my life forever. I realized that fatherhood is a great responsibility that I should accept. I grew up without a father because he died of a heart attack when I was 16 months old, and I know how much I missed by not having a father. I made a commitment to be there for my three children. I made sure that I was a role model for them by working hard and playing by the rules. I was also blessed with a good wife to be my partner.

The United States Department of Health and Human Services published the following information about the importance of fathers:

"Children who live with their biological fathers are, on average, at least two to three times more likely not to be poor, less likely to use drugs, less likely to experience educational, health, emotional and behavioral problems, less likely to be victims of child abuse, and less likely to engage in criminal behavior than their peers who live without their married, biological (or adoptive) parents. These differences are observed even after controlling for socioeconomic variables such as race and income" (http://fatherhood.hhs.gov/Parenting/index.shtml).

"Involved fathers provide practical support in raising children and serve as models for their development. Children with involved, loving fathers are significantly more likely to do well in school, have healthy self-esteem, exhibit empathy and pro-social behavior compared to children who have uninvolved fathers. Committed and responsible fathering during infancy and early childhood contributes emotional security, curiosity, and math and verbal skills"

(http://fatherhood.hhs.gov/).

I stayed involved in my children's lives and helped instill values in them. I read to them when they were little. I made sure I put them in many activities, such as Little League, dance, swimming, girl scouts, boy scouts, and Sunday school.

I helped them with homework and made sure I went to parent-teacher conferences and every school event they were involved in.

I disciplined them when necessary and stressed the importance of staying away from bad kids who broke the law and did unethical things. I think that by being involved in their lives, I made a positive difference. Too many fathers are "missing in action," and their children suffer because of it. Our country needs more involvement by fathers to strengthen and support the next generation.

I'm My Own Man

Harry Katopodis

School Teacher

Words from Mom

Demetrius Earl Zeigler was born on Friday, December 18, 1992, at 3:52 p.m. at William Beaumont Hospital in Royal Oak, Michigan. He was the 2nd child born to Nate and myself. Demetrius was on antibiotics at the age of two weeks, twice a day, until he was 4 years of age, because of his Sickle Cell beta-thalassemia disease. His dad carries the Sickle Cell trait, and I carry the thalassemia trait. At the age of three, he was diagnosed with asthma.

When he was younger, he was always going through emergency to get breathing treatments, even though he had a breathing machine at home. I would say the years from the age of 5 to 11 were the worst for his Sickle

Cell pain, which at the time was mainly in his legs and arms. Demetrius would be in so much pain that he would have to be carried or he would crawl around, because he couldn't put pressure on his legs.

Sickle Cell affects everyone differently. Demetrius has never been able to go swimming because the pressure of the water instantly cramps his legs. His dad was abusive to me, but when I kicked him out, I gave him every opportunity to spend time with his children; and he chose not to. Demetrius still has a relationship with his grandmother and his aunt on his dad's side. He just doesn't see his dad anymore.

Love you Demetrius,

MOM

Words from another Mom

My name is Elaine Foust Long and I am the editor of Demetrius's book. You might think that this is an odd place for an editor's page, but I am not just the editor. I am connected to three of the men who have stories printed in this book. One of the men is my life partner, another is my son, and the third is the son of my first husband. As you know, the world is full of people who have grown up without fathers. I am not one of them. My father was a loving, kind, and wonderful man, and he was one of the best role models for my three children who grew up in a fatherless home for most of their childhood. And the few years that they did have a father/stepfather, they were the most miserable years of their lives.

My children have different fathers. My first husband and I had twin girls. Our marriage did not last three years. He was very immature and was an alcoholic. He was really absent from his daughters' lives most of the time except for short spurts where he had a girlfriend who was interested in kids. They never seemed to last too long, though. I know that this book is about boys, but I wanted to mention something here about what a minister told me about my daughters not having their father in their lives.

I was so worried about them when they were little because I had such a close relationship with my father. I believed that they were missing out on so much and I asked this minister if he would talk to the girls for me. After he met with them and talked to them, he later told me that they did not have the problem. He told me that I had the problem. He said that the girls could not feel the absence of their father because they never really had him in their lives. Go figure! They got the love of an adult man through MY father. And they knew the unconditional love that I had for them.

So, I found that very interesting. But later I remarried and my second husband and I had a little boy together. Our marriage did not last but 7 years and he made my daughters' lives a living hell. Our son was too young when we split up to really have any feelings about the whole situation until he got a few years older. He really felt the sting of not having his father as a positive role model in his life. The difference was night and day between my daughters and my son.

As a person who has witnessed much of this kind of behavior from men in my life and in those lives that I come in contact with, I have come to the conclusion that most men do not have the parenting skills that women do. And many men didn't really want to have kids and they felt trapped when their women ended up pregnant. It is sad that this happens, but we need to do the best things for these innocent children who are born under these circumstances. And sometimes the best thing is to raise them without the negative parent in their lives.

It is not healthy to say that a lousy father is better than none at all. That just is not true. Lousy parents cannot show the love that every child needs. Lousy parents cannot teach children to be good adults; children learn by example. Perhaps it is a blessing when the bad parent goes away and never comes back.

This is where the role of the mother is so important. Mothers can try to replace the deadbeat dads by doing things with their sons that fathers usually do. I sat many a time with my son watching football games and baseball games. I sat with him and played with his sports cards and board games. We read together. We went on vacations together—just he and I. We had a lot of the same interests—he was my life. I stopped dating when he was 11 and started his counseling sessions. I needed to focus on him and keeping him healthy. I was there for him and I loved him unconditionally, even when he was angry and not so much fun to be around. I loved him when he walked out of school; I loved him when he was doing terrible things to our home. No matter what he did, I still loved him and never let him forget that.

The fact that he is now a happy and productive adult leads me to believe that my love pulled him through all of his bad times. When we danced together at his wedding, we had no words to say; we both just sobbed the whole time we danced that dance. I think that at that moment, we realized that we had made it!

So, if there are any mothers reading this book that have children who have lousy or deadbeat dads, don't try to force their fathers to spend time with them. The kids are better off without negative people in their lives. Be their mother and their father. You have it in you to love them enough for two people. Be firm and get your child support from them so you don't have to work 2 or 3 jobs to support them. The kids need you more than they need things.

And boys, don't dwell on the fact that your fathers are deadbeats or worthless, you have people in your life who do love and value you. Give these people the energy you spend hating your fathers or feeling sorry for yourselves. It is sad, yes, but they are the losers, because they don't have the pleasure of your smile, your respect, your love. You are valuable and you do not need a father to prove that. ***Be your own man!***

Part Two
The Boys' Stories

My Story
Living in an Abusive
Household

"About 40 percent of children in father-absent homes have not seen their father at all during the past year; 26 percent of absent fathers live in a different state than their children; and 50 percent of children living absent from their father have never set foot in their father's home"(Promoting 1).

What defines a man? What qualities do men have? I wonder how many men can actually consider themselves real men. Is it volunteering for Real Men Read Day or simply being a leader and allowing younger men to follow in your direction?

Oh, hello. There you are. I was just asking myself some questions about men. My name is Demetrius Zeigler, and this is my personal memoir, *Fatherless Sons*. I was born in Royal Oak, and raised in Highland Park, Michigan, by my strong mother. My dad, failed to be a part of my life. I live in a small city inside Detroit, Michigan.

I grew up on Third and Manchester in a town-house in the Gabrielle Community. Growing up with a dad abusing my mother and destroying my family has scarred me for life. Being raised by a single mother with no father has inspired me to be a big brother and a role model to young men like myself in father-absent homes. In the state of Michigan, young men in father-less homes have an increased risk of being incarcerated. This is a story about my life and how I became My Own Man.

Outside, there was dirt, rather than grass, a parking lot, and a playground right down the street. I had a lot of good friends that I used to play with outside. My sister and I both had mutual friends: KC, Ally, and SK, to name a few. Every day, we all would play outside, just enjoying what life had to offer. I remember some of our best times were when we all would go to the drive-in with my friend SK's mother. Man, going to the drive-in was in style back in the day. Well, at least it was to us. Before heading out, we would run to each other's homes and ask our parents if we all could go.

That's how I remember it being in my childhood neighborhood. We were all family. Each of our parents trusted each other, and allowed the others to take us places. I will never forget my childhood neighborhood and friends. Many people might think I had everything I needed—a mother, a dad, a sister, a home, friends, and a playground—but that was looking from the outside in, not from the inside.

My dad lived with us until I was aged nine. I always used to ask myself what I did wrong for him to leave us. Was I not good enough? Was I not really his child? Did I not fit into his expectations of what he wanted in a child? Was I not walking or talking like him, or acting how he wanted me to act? Every day, I asked myself these questions because I thought I had done something that made him mad. I thought I was the reason why he left us. Maybe he would have stayed if I wasn't playing video games and played catch with him outside instead. Maybe he would have stayed if I wasn't always sick or in the hospital suffering from Sickle Cell

Disease. But the questions I really wanted an answer to are these:

- How could a man walk out on his son knowing that he would need a proper education and the skills to grow up and become a real man?

- How could my father walk out on me, knowing that I looked up to him and that I wanted to follow in his footsteps?

To this day, I am still waiting for answers.

My dad became abusive to my mother. Every night I would hear screaming and banging on the floor, not knowing that the loud noise was coming from my mother being pushed down by my dad. As an eight-year-old kid, I really don't know how to react when I see my mother being hit by someone. All I remember was the crying and screaming from my mother, pleading for my dad to stop. Have you ever experienced seeing your dad beating on your mom and feeling hopeless? To me, it felt like a fire truck going to put out a fire without water or a hose: the feeling of being helpless.

I felt like just jumping right in the middle of it and stopping him. "Dad stop, Dad stop, Dad stop!" was all I was screaming. I remember running down stairs because I didn't want to hear it any longer; all of the screaming and crying, I couldn't take it anymore.

Day after day, night after night, my dad would fight with my mom. It was as if he was really trying to hurt her. I remember one school morning being awakened by screaming, only to find my dad lying on top of my mom. I felt so bad; I just wanted him to stop. The next day, my sister, my mother, my aunt and I went out for a drive, and my mother sat in the car and started crying. Her exact words were, "He keeps beating me."

Do you know how that makes me feel even today, knowing that because of my age, I was helpless? I wish I could have done something like called the police or gone for help, but all I could do was sit there and do nothing. The pain that was going through my body and mind was so intense.

My aunt would always say, "Everything will be okay; just continue to believe in God." I didn't really understand why she kept saying that. All I knew was that there had to be some reason why she kept repeating herself. My aunt would also say, "All you have to do is pray, pray, pray and your worries will go away." I just was so mad at my dad for putting his hands on a female, my mom.

To all young men reading this book: never put your hands on a female. You must learn how to walk away when you get angry. The key to solving problems is communication. You will lose respect as a man if you use violence. A lesson that I learned from my dad was not to do what he did: destroy a home.

After a few weeks went by, I remember my dad wanted to come back into my life. Now, after everything that had happened, why would he want to come back? Did your other family not want you anymore? Did they leave him because he was about to destroy their home too? I didn't understand why he wanted to come back into our lives after my mom finally put him out. My dad didn't deserve my mother. People always used to say that, "One man's trash is another man's treasure." One day, my mother will be loved again.

My dad failed me, but my mom and God saved me. My mother is my rock, my life, and my heart. I love my mother so much and will never let another man do anything bad to hurt her.

Mom, you are a strong fighter, who fought for many years of your life just to protect us and save your marriage. Well, now it's my turn to protect you and my family. It's my turn to provide the necessities that are needed to run a home.

Even though my dad failed to raise me as a man, I am a real man, and have my GOD and mother to thank for that. Thank you for teaching me what my dad didn't. Thank you for protecting me and not walking out on me. I love you both so much! If it wasn't for you both, I couldn't imagine where I would be standing today. Would I be a school dropout, or incarcerated, or just another statistic?

My mother used to babysit children from the neighborhood to make the money she needed to continue to support our family and put food on the table. She also did it because it was something she loved doing. I remember one time my mother was babysitting a few of us children and the doorbell rang. You know how children are; we were all yelling "Doorbell! Doorbell!"

and running up to my mother saying, "Someone is at the door, Mom."

My mom went to look out the peephole to see who it was, and from her facial expression, I knew it was somebody she didn't want to see. Me being very hyper, I ran to the kitchen window and tried to see who it was. Of course, as children, we didn't know how to sneak and look out the window, so we opened all the blinds and put our faces against the glass.

It was at that very moment that I saw my dad walking off the porch. I was scared. I didn't know what to say. I heard banging at the back window. My mother told all the children to go into the kitchen and be very quiet. My dad heard us and knew we were in the house, but I guess he didn't understand why we were not answering the door.

Bang! The basement glass window was busted out. At this point, I just knew he was going to catch us and hurt us. My mother grabbed as many children as she could and told us all to run as fast as we could down the street to her friend's house. All I can remember was doing exactly what my mother told me to do, running as fast as I could all the way down the street.

A few minutes later, the police arrived, but my dad was long gone. After that, I was so scared to even sleep in my own bed. I was so scared, I asked my mother to take me over to my grandmother's house, so I could feel safer. My sister and I stayed over at my grandmother's house for a couple of days, just to feel better and not be scared anymore. To this day, I remember everything that happened. Why would he do that? Why would he come and scare his children like that? Why would he try to destroy our family again?

After coming back home from my grandmother's house, I started to have different types of dreams. When I say different, I mean scary. I had dreams of my dad cursing me out and saying that he didn't love me anymore. I had a dream about my dad marrying a different woman and starting a new family. Dream after dream, night after night, I couldn't sleep, tossing and turning all night long, hearing that bang of the basement window in my head. Some nights I would slide on the floor and crawl under my bed because I had a feeling that my dad was coming back.

After my dad left our family, my mom and my sister and I all began to struggle. We did not struggle alone; however, we struggled together. We were one big family, united. My mom struggled to keep food on the table and clothes on our backs. I used to cry myself to sleep every night, not knowing if we would be able to eat the next day. Some people may think that kids should be playing with their friends and not worrying about these kinds of things; but when your mother is struggling, no matter how old you are, you have to stand strong and help her.

Some things always used to upset me, such as when my friends talked about how great their fathers were, how much their fathers were doing for them. Being young, I never knew there were actually great fathers in this world that didn't walk out on their children, leaving them with nothing and destroying their home. If you are a father reading this, please love your children. Teach your son or sons how to grow up and become "real men." Most important, teach them to respect women.

To all young men, I say that not having a father is not the time to be falling apart; it's a time to pull yourself together, because you are responsible for keeping your family together and protected. Not having a father in my life has motivated me to do bigger and better things. My dad has motivated me to go through life with my head held high, feeling confident in myself because

"I'm My Own Man."

My Teen Years

As I entered middle school at Henry Ford Academy in Highland Park, Michigan, my grades started to slip. I think it was because of my dad walking out on us. I know what you all are thinking: "What a poor excuse."

Believe me; I used to get all good grades until I started to feel lonely. There is something about the relationship between a dad and a son, something that a mother cannot provide. Dads and sons connect in a certain way that mothers and daughters will never understand. A son connects with his dad because he knows that his dad will always protect him from everything. I guess I just never had the chance to connect with my dad. He left me too soon. We never did anything together. He wasn't a good dad to me or my sister, nor was he a good husband to my mother.

Understand the difference between a dad and a father. A father is a man who takes care of his children and family with no questions asked. Any fool can be a dad, but it takes a real man to be a FATHER! So, to all the young men, I say: "You want to be a father, not a dad." That's why you always hear females say, "Deadbeat dad" and never "Deadbeat father." The idea of a deadbeat father just doesn't make any sense.

I began to think that my Sickle Cell could have been the real reason why my dad never acknowledge us anymore; but that only makes his actions worse—leaving children who are hurting and hopeless. My dad always used to be gone from home. Was he really at work? Was he out cheating? Question after question ran through my head; all I wanted were answers.

Anyway, sorry for kind of falling off track, but back to my education. At Henry Ford Academy, I was one of the top students, but soon that all came to an end. Grades didn't matter anymore to me, and teachers didn't matter to me either. The only thing that I was thinking about in school was how my life was so messed up. Kids used to tease me all the time about stupid things. They used to make fun of me just to make their friends laugh.

Why would someone talk about another human being like that just to impress their friends? Guys, you do not know the different situations teenagers might be in. They may be having a very bad day. Whatever the situation is, my point is simple: "Don't use a human life to impress friends." Those students in my school were unaware of what I was going through, but I forgive them. You must forgive in order to forget, young men. After everything that has happened, I now forgive my dad. I'm done with this chapter in my life. Now it's time to open a new one.

Challenging Yourself

Have you ever had the mindset that you were out to destroy your self-image? Were your priorities of good grades and school set aside in order to fulfill your immature desires? In high school, there were times when I didn't take my work as seriously as I should have. My first two years in high school, classwork was the least of my priorities. Having fun and going to school activities were all I cared about. Homecoming, football games, baseball and basketball games, and even parades and school dances were some of the major events at my school. There was just so much to do at school; I couldn't let all of that go to waste.

I had such a stupid mindset in high school. I remember my school principal calling me to her office for a meeting. Was I in trouble or did she have something nice for me? As I walked in her office, she told me to close the door and sit down at the table. She said, "At the beginning of the year, I told every student that we had a policy that, to stay in the program, students had to maintain a 2.5 GPA." I began to look around, thinking to myself, "Like you have the wrong person because I know I still have over a 2.5 GPA." I responded by saying, "Um, I thought I had over a 2.5 GPA. What is my GPA?" "Your GPA is 2.0," she responded.

I was hoping that she was joking because I already knew my mother would punish me for getting low grades. Not only did I have a 2.0 GPA, but I was getting all Cs and sometimes Ds. My principal didn't kick me out of the program, but she put me on academic probation for a few weeks. I felt really bad, but after the meeting, I challenged myself. I challenged myself to get off academic probation, to get a 3.0 GPA, and to improve all my bad grades.

I was very foolish, having imagined that just because the teachers knew me and would joke around with me, they were going to give me a good grade without any work effort. SILLY ME! See, this is the problem many students in high school have. They think that just because the teacher likes them and jokes around with them, that they are going to get good marks and pass along to the next grade. Such students think that high school is just a big joke, but it really isn't. Some kids even skip class and joke around to impress their friends. They need to wake up because it doesn't work like that. I had to find out the hard way.

High school and college are two different things, two different businesses. College is a "big test," to use my own words. To me, it's there to test for Maturity and Responsibility, the two key factors of college and success. Without them, you will be lost and will fail; but with them, trust me, you will succeed and be all you can be. College is a place to network for the near future, but you should always remember that it is also the place where you will receive a higher education than in high school. To me, college is the best, and I love it. It has helped me grow as a man. I take on so much responsibility every day to the point that I love being on campus.

College is life. GO TO COLLEGE, MEN, PLEASE. Not just young men, but young ladies, too.

It is so important to broaden your horizon. Young men, even if you don't care about anything I have said in my book so far, just promise me that you will CHALLENGE YOURSELF! Challenge yourself to pass every class and every test.

Challenge yourself to never give up or drop out. I have had the experience of seeing my friends walk through the high school door in ninth grade, but never make it to graduation. I also have had the opportunity to watch many friends start their first year of college and not make it to their sophomore year. Challenge yourself to graduate and help somebody else along the way. Challenge yourself to succeed in life and become all that you can be.

You can be anything in the world. If nobody in your life ever told you that they believe in you, let me be the first: "I BELIEVE IN YOU 100%." I love you, my young brothers, sisters, and future leaders in life. Many young men seem to not care about anything or anybody around them. It's like they cut off society and opportunity from connecting with them. To be honest, that's exactly how I felt when I was younger, but now I have overcome that barrier in my life, and you all must too. Challenge yourself to succeed so we can each say, "I'm My Own Man."

Leviticus 19:18 says, "You shall not take vengeance or bear a grudge against the sons of your own people, but you shall love your neighbor as yourself: I am the Lord."

The American Justice Department's bullying statistics show that one out of every four kids will be bullied sometime throughout their adolescence. About 42 percent of kids have been bullied while online, with one in four being verbally attacked more than once. According to the I-Safe American Survey of Students Bullying Statistics, about 58 percent of kids admit to never telling an adult when they've been the victim of a bullying attack.

Why do I care? Like many other adolescents, I too was a victim of bullying. I was a student at one of the middle schools in my neighborhood. I found myself being victimized by another young man. This guy was huge compared to the average middle school student. To pick my brain a little bit more, this dude had to be about 5"9, 295 pounds minimum. I mean, this dude was huge. I remember everyday bringing money to school just to give to him. He directed me to sit in front of him every day in every class. I remember days when he would talk about me in my face, to make other students laugh. Fat, ugly, stupid, King Kong, monkey, gorilla, and gay—those were the names I endured.

Being verbally bullied not only happened in middle school, but continued during my high school career. In high school, some of the male jocks always called me gay or fag.

There were certain hallways and classrooms I avoided because I was afraid I would be judged. I found myself never going into lunch rooms because that's where all of the jocks hung out. I walked down hallways with my head down, which became a habit. I never went to gym classes, male assemblies, or anything else where I would be bullied. It was crazy that these students, my fellow classmates, put this label on me, a label that stamped me gay, when I knew I wasn't.

My biggest regret about being bullied is that I allowed it to happen for 6 years. I should have spoken up. Even though I am a statistic of being bullied, I thank God I am not a statistic of teen suicide due to bullying. If you are a victim of any type of bullying, speak up. Tell someone, a teacher, principal, neighbor, or a friend, so you can get help. You see I did it, I told you.

Being bullied in high school, I thought I would never amount to anything. I ended up challenging myself to get out of that situation, and I did. One of the biggest things I did was speaking up for myself. After I spoke up for myself, the bullying stopped, and everything in my life changed. I challenged myself to become a role model to the guys that victimized me. I wanted to show them that there was more to bullying and trying to impress their friends. I joined Student Government, Robotics team, The Detroit Urban Debate League, and in my senior year, I was elected as President of the Class of 2011. You too can speak up if you're being bullied. But, don't just speak up, forgive them, and become a role model to them.

Luke 6:37 says, "Judge not, and ye shall not be judged: condemn not, and ye shall not be condemned: forgive, and ye shall be forgiven:"

No truer words were ever written. I live my life with this thought in mind. If more people would do this, there would be a pretty decent chance for world peace.

In Retrospect

Looking back at growing up without my father, there were times when I really missed not having a father in my life. Some holidays were very difficult, especially when we would go to my grandmother's house for Christmas. (His mother). All of my aunts and cousins would be there, but my father never showed up. I kept looking for him to come, but he never did. Eventually I stopped looking for him. No point in watching for someone who is never going to come.

He missed out on all of the important times in my life: birthdays, holidays and all of my graduations— not even a personal visit, just for the heck of it. There were no father-son banquets, sports, never came to any music concerts where I played several different instruments. He was a father in name only. He never made a point to love me or share in my life.

I did have male role models, however. My uncles always treated me well; and Uncle Bennie treated me like I was his own, and I thank him for that!

There was one person who was most like a father to me and that is my mother. She loves me enough for two parents. She did not want me to go through life wounded because of the pain my father inflicted on both of us. My mother tried to make up for his absence. We did everything together. This helped me sometimes to not even miss my father's presence.

I have learned a lot from my mother. She taught me to always be responsible for my actions, but most important, she taught me to fight for what is right. I would have to say that watching my mother fight for many years of her life helped to contribute to my success in life so far. I learned to be grateful, and to be happy with whatever I have in life. We often miss out on precious memories of the things we have because we are too focused on what we do not have.

And my mother taught me to respect women and myself. She taught me how to love and she taught me parenting skills that I will take forward with me to my future family. I promise my future family that I will love them unconditionally, I will show them kindness, and I will protect them with all that I am.

I have learned so much from the people who love me. I learned responsibility from my mother; I learned the true meaning of kindness from my Grandmother Hardy. My granny on my dad's side is special to me because she never left my or my sister's side when my dad walked out on us. She taught us to always love one another no matter what the situation is.

My uncles, David, Rick, James, Byron, Matthew, Dominic, Frank, Kenneth, Bennie, Willie—they all taught me the real definition of a man. My aunts, Evelyn, Yvette, Lanette, Lafondra, Sharon, Cynthia, Mevelyn, Telisha, Nicole—they all loved and accepted me for who I am. My sister Ciara, my cousins, and the whole family taught me to love myself.

Having such a wonderful and close family has brought me to the point where I am today.

God, I'm Letting It Go

To be honest I was hurt when my dad walked out on me. There were so many different emotions running through my body, but I didn't want to talk to my mom about it. My dad really left me. I wanted to grow up and be like my dad. Walk like him and talk like him. I wanted to marry a wonderful woman, just like he did. The pain was so deep. I wanted a father to protect me from bullies and enemies, to protect me from all types of violence, and help me with my homework when I came home from school. Dad, you were supposed to take me shopping for my mom on Mother's Day. I wanted you to teach me right from wrong and how to stand on my two feet and defend myself. You were supposed to love me and forgive me when I did something wrong. I wish we could have gone to basketball games. I wanted to open my birthday gifts with you.

I wanted a father to heal my pain when I was hurt. You were supposed to be the father to watch me grow up from child to teenager to adult. I wanted you to come to see me graduate from middle school, high school, and college. I was so hurt about everything that happened, but I must say that my past is over now. I forgive you, Dad, for everything you did. I forgive you for not being a father to me and for leaving me. You divorced your wife, but you weren't supposed to divorce your children.

God, I Let It Go!   I am my own man.

Daniel's Story

My name is Daniel. I never really had a dad; unless you call the man my mom married my dad. His name was Frank. I never really knew my dad due to him being incarcerated throughout my childhood.

My mom did the best she could with me and my brother. I met my supposed-to-be father through a jail cell door where he had no idea who my brother and I were. I was only 12 years old when I met my dad; and quite frankly, I didn't know who he was. My mom dated a lot of men in her lifetime. I called them all "Dad" not even knowing which the real one was.

Growing up and being raised by my mom half of my life, not knowing who my real dad was, made my life hard. Living with my mom was not easy, even though I knew my mom did what she did to take care of us. But that was a hard life. Getting beaten, hit with bats, broom sticks, hammers and getting kicked out was a life I just didn't want to have.

When I was little, I tried numerous times to commit suicide because my life was horrible; and not having a father made me feel lost in society. Being raised by my mom, I don't know if she did it to better the cause, but one night, I was sent to the hospital because my mom kicked me out and left me in the cold for three days straight and never came to look for me.

My Mom said that we needed to spend time with my dad, so she sent us to Michigan to live. My mom sent us on the bus at the age of 15 with little to no money. During the bus ride, my brother and I often got hungry, so we started stealing from local corner stores. This was the first time I ever stole anything in my life; I was only 15. Don't get me wrong, as I look back on my actions, I understand that what I did was illegal, but I had to find some way to survive. For hours of the trip, I felt sick. I was sick to my stomach because not only did my dad abandon us, but now my mom did too. I didn't know what would happen when we reached Michigan. Would my dad meet us at the bus station? Or would my brother and I become victims of abandonment?

We arrived at the bus terminal in Michigan, and Frank, my dad, was standing there and said "Welcome home." I had moved so much during my childhood, I thought everywhere was home because I never really had one. "Dad" is what I called him.

I was young, what else could I say. I was a little frightened when we went to his home, because it was as if I was walking with a stranger. Should I forgive him for leaving us, or has he even forgiven himself? He used to tell me and my brother, that he wanted to get to know us better. He said .....He wanted to love us more.

I was so blinded when he said he loved us and wanted to be family. For a split second, I almost believed him. There I was again, lost. I didn't know if I should love him, or better yet, trust him. I didn't want my heart to be left in the hands of a thief.

My mom said that we were double trouble, but in my eyes, we were kids. It's like he was our dad to abuse us and take his anger out on my brother and me. It was like living in hell; then he sent us back to Mom's. As a child I never got a chance to have fun, you know, be a kid.

As a child, I used to get called names like bastard because I didn't know my dad. Being a child or kid without a father, could you imagine how career day was, looking at all the other kids' fathers who were talking about their jobs? Just them being there was like it was tearing me apart because I was there all alone with no dad.

Mom was always at work so my brother and I never saw her that much. To be honest, it was like she was never there. So really my brother and I, at a young age, had to become our "own men" and watch out for each other. My mom tried to make sure we were in a nice place to live where there was a lower crime rate.

Right until I was up to the age of 15, my mom sent us back to Detroit to stay this time. She said we need to spend more time with our dad. I'm 15, almost 16; now you want to show up!! I thought to myself. I got in the car; it was quiet. But I couldn't blame him, because my mom wasn't telling the truth about my real father.

So in my mind as a 15-year-old child, any man that was taking care of me was my father. Being young, I really didn't know any better; I just thought that my life would be better than it was in South Carolina. New life, new people; my life started out pretty good, living with him.

I was a young man, finally having a father that was doing his duties as a man. It made me happy; it filled that empty space in my heart. I started school in the 8th grade; my brother was in the 7th grade, he had to stay back because he wasn't doing what he supposed to.

I graduated the 8th grade, and started high school. My father told me I should play sports, so I joined the wrestling team, tried football—but that didn't work out. So I was a wrestler and had my first match. My dad came to the match. I was happy to see him there, so I was going to show off, even though I lost. That's when my brother and I became closer than ever.

Going home was like a nightmare that I didn't want to be in. Sometimes it was fun, but other times I was missing my mom. But I didn't want to suffer up there, because I guess he gave us whatever we wanted. Well, almost, but it felt like it was temporary. That's what I thought it was, but his mother used to take care of us.

My first homecoming, I'm expecting my dad to cash me out. As a kid, I didn't care about the value of money. His mother gave him the money to send me to get fitted for my suit. My two years being there weren't all they were cracked up to be. We were young kids being kids, because we didn't get to do the things we got to do when we first came here.

Instead of talking to us like a father to sons, it was like he took his anger out on us. Being punched in the chest, choking us up, sometimes his mother used to have to come stop him because he got too carried away with the beatings. It felt like we were slaves; like I was dying. He used to tell me and my brother that he didn't want us to be afraid of him—that we could talk to him about anything. Not only could we not talk to him, but he put fear in our hearts.

I always tried to bring home A's and Bs because anything lower than that, we were going to get "beat up." That's what it seemed like to me. I'm not saying my brother and I were angels, but we were young; we didn't have a man in our lives to tell us what is right and what is wrong. No young man should experience anything like what we went through.

Our 16th birthday came, and we had so much fun; we went everywhere. I almost forgot about the things he used to do to us that kind of felt like love. Really, I didn't know if he was just trying to make up for what he did, but he can't buy happiness with money; he can't buy his way into my heart. Sometimes I wanted to tell him, "If you are my father, then where have you been all my life? Why did you have us thinking that we were alone, and why did I have to find out about you at the age of 12?"

My 10th grade year started off ugly: a custody battle. My mom wanted us back, but my brother and I were tired of moving around. We just wanted to stay and finish school first. At the end of my 10th grade year, my mom tried to come back and get us; but she was just trying to take us away from him. She called the cops on Frank, who was supposed to be the father of two boys.

What made me believe that he wasn't my father, and he was just like the rest of them? So my mom told him to take a DNA test, and he refused to take it. He says "If they are not mine, I took care of them like they were mine." To me, that was no reason not to take it.

However, my mom ended up taking us back with her; we were supposed to be down there for 2 months, for the whole summer. They used to fight all the time and when he talked about my mom, he talked about her so bad. Sometimes I couldn't even stand in front of him while he was talking like she was nothing. It hurt a lot, but I always said "I'll never talk about your mom in a bad way."

So we went to Georgia to start our summer, at least I thought so. I found out that my mom was sick, but I didn't hear it from her. When I found out, it tore my heart into pieces, because my mom kept it from us for so long. I thought I was losing my mom. She had a tumor and breast cancer.

Knowing what my mom was going through was breathtaking. It felt like the devil was trying to take my mother. I almost lost my faith in God because I thought I was losing my mom. Being there and watching her go through that pain and not being able to do anything about it was unbearable. My mom kept trying to get me to stay, but I was still in school. I just wanted to stay in one place and finish school because I was always moving

It was almost time for us to go back to Michigan. One night, like three days before the time for me to go, I found out my momma had a kidney stone. So it's the day I have to go back; my brother wanted to stay behind, and I didn't want him to stay. But he wanted to be by Mom's side; we had never been separated. It hurt not having my brother on that bus with me.

My mom was mad, but we were supposed to go back together. We had to go to school. When I got on the bus, I couldn't even look back and see my brother wave goodbye because it hurt so much. As I got on the bus, I thought a lot about getting off; but I couldn't, we were already going.

After I got back, Frank found out that my brother didn't come back on the bus with me. I told him why my brother didn't come back, and he made his choices. A couple of months passed and I started to notice that my supposed father was fading away slowly from me.

I was not seeing him very often and he lived only a couple blocks away.

School started and I found out I made it to the 11th grade. As the school year went on, it felt like he just left my life. My brother called and told me he was in some trouble and I'm like, "Man, I haven't even been there 90 days, and you got in to some kind of mess." He said that some kids blamed him for selling weed in school and when the cops came to check his locker and stuff, they didn't find anything; but yet, they still put him on probation. I told him he should have come home like he was supposed to.

He was feeling it, but I told him not to worry. When I told my father, he already knew; but he never went to go get my brother out of that mess and bring him back home. Instead he left him there. Frank started hanging out with his girlfriend and her kids more than he did me, his own child.

Frank used to tell me that he'll never do what his father did to him. But to me, it felt like they were all lies; I didn't know who to believe. My momma started saying that he wasn't my father. For so long, she had been telling me that he was. So in the back of my head, I had doubts if he really was or not.

I think about the past every day, how my dad used to beat us. I watched my supposed-to-be father punch my brother and me. He choked my brother on the stairs one time, and my brother started calling my name, saying that he can't breathe. I wanted to hit Frank because he was taking his anger out on him for no reason. But I knew I wasn't going to win, so all I could do was push him off; and he said that he wasn't choking him. I asked him "What type of father does that to his kids to teach them something?"

Frank and I fell apart when my brother left, even though we were never close. If anyone ever asked me to name some good things about my father, I wouldn't even know what to say. Watching him taking care of Britany and her kids was too much for me to watch. I used to think that I was invisible to him, like I was a knot in his belt or a waste of space or if I even existed in his world.

Coming home, he use to talk about how much he helped people to get in school, how he would write them letters of recommendation. But as his son, he stopped being there for me. I asked myself why? Why wasn't he ever there, why did he stop coming around; was it because he knew he wasn't my father, or was he ashamed to tell me the truth. Never having a father to be there through your dark moments and mom always being at work took a toll on me; but I asked God to help me through it; far as I know, He is my father figure.

As time went on, I realized some things never change. As 11th grade went on, I still felt fatherless. I was that kid who played a lot, and tried to smile to hide the pain I was going through by feeling alone. I used to think no one knew what I was going through; not having my brother there beside me felt like the other half of my heart was crushed.

Through my whole teenage life, I had to become my own man and take up for myself because every time I talk to him about things going on in my life, it's like he doesn't care about it. I had to be my own man because he stopped being there for me in the 11th grade.

My grandmother, his mom—I love her to death because she was the one who was really taking care of me and my brother. Still going through being a fatherless son, living in a world like this, makes you not want it. I mean, he only lived a few minutes away from his mother, and he can't even come by to check on her. So I knew from that point on, that if not seeing his mother like that, what makes you think he is going to see his son?

I was still in high school, I barely can take care of myself, and he left me here at my granny's house for me to watch and look after her. But I had my own life; one day I told him, "No disrespect, but this not my momma; this is my grandmother." He got mad at me for that, but I was being honest; I had my own life to live.

Every time I used to go somewhere with my friends, he'd call and ask where I was and I'd tell him, he'd get mad and ask why I was not at home. He'd ask me why I was leaving his mother at home by herself. But it was his mother, not mine. He didn't care; so I really had no life, no friends. It felt like I couldn't do anything, like I was being used.

It was my senior year in high school which was every child's dream because you are at that point where you are almost done. My senior year started off sad because someone told me they heard my brother got locked up, and I didn't believe it.

I finally talked to my brother. I could tell he was scared because I felt his pain. I mean, we are twins. He didn't know how to take it, but he didn't want me to go see him like that. Till this day, I haven't seen my brother's face, only pictures. My dad didn't help me get over the pain; he just left it alone and said that TJ did what he did, so he had to do the time. I know that, but that's your son.

My brother had a son; he was telling me about this girl named Jessica who was pregnant with his baby. My brother will never get to see his son's first birthday or even see him grow up.

I started to turn to the wrong people for love and support because I wasn't getting it from my father. My grades started dropping in school. I thought about dropping out. My vocal music teacher was my only friend in school; he saw something in me that my dad didn't even see in me. He got me back on the right track. I started getting better at sports, and my grades were ok.

Seniors dues were due—money that we have to pay basically to walk across the stage. Coming home from school, Frank was there talking to his mother. I opened the door and I told everyone "Hey." He didn't say anything; I gave him the paper that was in my hand. My granny asked what it was; she so nosey. I told her it was my senior dues that I have to pay to walk across the stage.

I handed the paper to my dad; he got up looked at it for a minute then put it back down and told his mother he'll see her later and just walked out of the house. I told my granny ok, so that must mean he's not going to pay it. My granny told me not to worry that he is going to pay it.

The first payment came up and I didn't even see my father that whole day, so how am I going pay my dues? I called him to ask him if he was going to give me the first payment; he never answered the phone. It hurt me when he did that; and he says he is my father! I couldn't believe it. I never saw him that whole week, so my granny took some money out of her wallet and gave me my first payment, and told me she'll pay for my dues.

One thing about him is that he does things on his own time; when he sees fit, it's supposed to be done. When my dad found out that she was helping me pay the dues, he got mad at her; it's like he didn't want me to succeed in life. So from that point on, I just thanked my granny for being there for me like she was. All through my senior she was the one who basically got me through high school. So I had no father in my eyes.

I had my life set on where I wanted to go to school. When Frank did come around, he would always give me a speech about life, and he was always talking about how he just helped out other people.

I put God first in everything I do. I keep a smile on my face, going to school not knowing who I am, really. Put yourself in my shoes, it'll seem like it was all a fairytale to be honest. As the months passed, my granny was still paying off my dues for me. I love her always, and I thank God that I have her in my life.

It came time in high school where we take our senior trip. My grandmother finished paying my dues. She also gave me money and sent me on my own senior trip. Before I left, she told me not to stay. I laughed!! And said "Thank you, I love you."

I left, headed down the road and caught the Greyhound bus. I was headed to Ohio to visit my cousins. Camille and her sons came to pick me up when I got there. She took me out and we had so much fun, I almost forgot about the pain of not having a father or not knowing who he was. I watched my cousin's husband; Billy was his name. I watched him with his kids; just watching that made me smile and hurt at the same time. Because I wished that I had a father growing up.

Later that day, I talked to my cousin and her husband. They were asking me about school, and did I do my FASFA, which school, etc. I had to tell the truth, and I told them: "You know my dad is not helping me, you know my federal aid is not done because I have to wait on him. Bill told me that when I graduate, I may come stay with them and I could go to school.

But the thought of leaving my granny was so painful. I missed my chance because I had no one to guide me down the right path. When I got back to Michigan, I decided to do for myself, to become a young man. As I got older, I finally realized that things were going to have to be done my way; no one else was trying to help me get to where I wanted to go. I never had a leader,

I told myself, and I needed to stop depending on my father.

If I ever make it big in life I want to tell him "thank you because you made me a man without raising me to become one. I learned from your mistakes and became a better father to my son than you were to me and I'm going to always be there for him. I wake up every morning wishing my life was better than what it is now, but I *will* succeed with or without you."

I'm 21 years of age and a man; and I'm proud to say it. I'm older and wiser and have my own little man, and I'm going to be the best father there is to him and never leave; and I'm going to still chase my singing dreams because music is the only thing that keeps me at peace. I hope one day my father will realize what he has done to me; but by that time, I think it'll be too late. For all the young men out there without a father, you are not alone. Just be strong, because you can make it without him; I did.

My name is Daniel and I'm My Own Man.

Robert's Story

Robert's story is a bit different than some of the others. He is a 60-year-old man who is from another country. Robert was brought here by his mother from Bavaria, Germany, along with his two younger brothers. It was the mid-60s and she brought her three sons to America to find a better life than they had in post-war Germany. She was a single mother, and she had a very difficult time settling in with her boys.

Robert's father had nothing to do with him until he was in his teens. By then, it was too late for him to be any kind of role model to him because he was seldom around. When Robert came to the United States, he was only 11 years old. He spoke no English and he suffered a lot of bullying from the other kids for different things. Since the war had been so recent, there was still many bad feelings about Hitler and the atrocities of the war, and ignorant people equated all Germans with Hitler. They also made fun of his accent and his poor knowledge of the English language.

After two years of being so unhappy here, his mother found a way to send him back to Germany to live with his grandparents. Robert lived on the farm with his grandparents and some of the aunts and uncles, so the family unit was large and close.

His father had always paid support to his mother, but his absence was rarely felt because it is pretty hard to miss something (or someone) you never really had. Robert had many male relatives in his life as role models. He also had a very strong and loving mother who was an integral part of his life.

When he was a teenager, his natural father made his appearance and wanted to get to know his son. He made a few attempts to do some things with Robert, but it just didn't click. And when Robert had finished high school in Germany, he came back to America to spend some time with his mother and brothers.

Now that he was a grown-up (19 years old), he found a job, made some friends, and he never went back to Germany to live. He has been in Maryland for 41 years. His father passed away some time ago. His mother met a kind man who married her and helped her to take care of her boys, but at this point Robert did not need a father figure as he was a grown man. His step-father was a person whom Robert looked up to and respected. He also has since passed away.

Robert was unfortunate enough to be unable to have any children, so he is not able to look at father-hood realistically. He recently met a woman who has 3 grown children and 13 grandchildren, so he is able to relate a little bit as an Opa (grandfather). And he is a really good grandfather to them. They adore him.

He admits that it would have been nice to have had a father to do things with—like motorcycles and cars, but he looks at the things that he *did* have. He had a mother who took good care of her boys, found a kind man to love her and her boys, and a close family.

And he is his own man.

David's Story

Let me start off by saying I believe he was one of the great men of the 20th century.

I am not going to tell you that he was perfect, because he wasn't; but I think that's the beauty of being a father. You don't have to be perfect; you just have to care enough to try. And just being available and receptive counts for so much.

The dynamic of our relationship is that my dad was already 49 years old when I was born, so unlike my relationship with little David. There is no going to baseball practice (where I now am one of the assistant coaches) or taking me off to bowling every week.

Our relationship was mostly watching sports together or television when he was home; I remember he worked the afternoon shift, and the words I mostly would hear were "I am telling your daddy when he gets home." That in itself would straighten out a lot of mess. Oh yes, I got whippings, and so did little Dave Jr. I got my last whipping as an 8th grader. So that is when Dave Jr. got his last whipping.

A father's job is to lay down the law. Let moms do all that talking; when that's over, its time to dispense some justice. Fathers have to do what they say they are going to do. No one watches you more closely than your son. I didn't whip him just to whip him. But I am a firm believer in if you don't whip your children when they need it, someone else will later in life; whether it be the court system or not.

The greatest advice he gave me was do more than one thing well; he said in this world you never know how things will go. So you better be able to provide for yourself and your family. If you can only do one thing, they may take that from you, and then what have you got?

He taught me patience and sacrifice, things you will need in all walks of life. He taught me how to catch fish and how to clean them. I learned discipline from him.

The things I am most proud of is that he loved the Lord, every chance he got he brought his family close, and he never met a stranger.

I thank God for My Dad and believe that I will be a successful parent if I can continue to share half the knowledge he bestowed on me.

I am my own man.

David Hardy

December 31 2013

John's Story

John was born into a family that included his mother, his father, and three half-sisters. His sisters were nine and fourteen years older than he was, so you can pretty much guess that he was a wee bit spoiled. John's father was a jock when he was in high school, wrestling and playing soccer. He really did not have much of a relationship with his daughter from his first marriage. He met his second wife who had twin daughters. They married and became a new little family.

John's parents were hoping for a little boy to complete their family, so they were delighted to find out that they had their little son. John's dad was so proud of having his dream come true, that he just had to call his ex-girlfriend to tell her all about his little boy. Wasn't that nice of him?

So, the happy little family played house for a few years. It seemed to be very difficult for Dad to deal with the kids. His job took him away four to five days a week, traveling around the northeastern states. He was in the auto industry, visiting the car dealers and helping them. When he came home on the weekends, he took to drinking a case of wine; this was for him to be able to deal with the kids and the noise that goes along with three kids. His wife worked evenings as a bartender for extra money so they could have extras.

While she was at work, daddy dearest was trying to win step-daddy of the year awards, by spanking his step-daughters as often as he could. Mom had decided years ago that she was not going to spank her children. She specifically told him that she did not want him spanking any of the kids. She asked him not to discipline the girls other than sending them to their room until she got home. After he spanked them anyway, he warned them that if their mother knew that they made him angry enough that he had to spank them, she would be really mad. So, they never told her about the spankings.

John apparently got some of the spankings too. But some of his more special memories of his father included having to watch his father build a bonfire and burn the toys that the three-year-old little boy did not pick up in his room. Nice dad. The twins were so upset that they called their mother at work and told her what he was doing. She told them that she would take care of that when she got home. Yes, there was a huge fight.

This man who held a 2-year associate's degree in psychology was totally clueless. All he did was whine about everything. Who broke this, who did that, why is this here? And so on. He refused to do family things because they were undoubtedly going to be fiascos. The poor twins could not ever do anything right. Because John was so little, the girls got the brunt of the anger he had to unleash.

Finally, mom got really tired of all the whining and complaining and she told him that she and the kids were leaving. He acted like he didn't believe that she would do it, but she did. Now he wanted to go for family counseling—what she had been asking him to do for years. But it was too late now. She had no love left for this man who was so unkind to her children. She packed up her three children and moved from a beautiful house on the side of a mountain to an apartment complex in the same school district. Her kids were never happier.

John was in kindergarten when they left his father. They moved about 5 miles away. Whenever John would go to visit his father, he would have to amuse himself while his dad worked out in the yard and woods. He never did 'dad and son things' with John. Most of the time, John did not want to go to his father's house. But his mother was going to college to get a better job and have nice things for the kids. She needed his dad to help out so she could work on the weekends. After she was finished with college, she did not force John to go to his dad's.

One time, his father actually told his mother that he couldn't get John every week or his third marriage was going to go down the tubes. Nice guy. John had a lot of anger inside of him. He became withdrawn, and started doing very poorly in school. His mother began taking him to counseling. When he first started, he was

11 years old, and he had a young male counselor. He met with John and his mother for a few months. His assessment was that John felt rejected by his father. He was angry. The counselor said that he wanted to meet with John's father. So "Dad" went along with him to his session.

After meeting with his dad only one time, the counselor told both John and his mother that after meeting John's father, he did not think that John would ever have a good relationship with him. He was too selfish. And the counselor also told John that his relationship with his mother was very good and that he should nurture that relationship, and he should not focus on his father.

Of course, telling that to a boy his age really did not help the situation. John's mother tried to compensate for his not having a father in his life. What little time that John saw of his father was not quality time. She was the one who sat and watched ball games with him. She was the one who played games and spent time with him. They did special things together. They could tell what the other was thinking most of the time. His mother was his father too. So, here was this young man, his father was 5 miles away, and he could have been 5 states away.

When John was 15 years old, he was still in counseling, only with an older woman this time. John was still an angry boy. One evening at his counseling session, he went in first to meet with her, and then she called in his mother. She told his mother to take him out to the hospital and contact crisis intervention, and she wanted him admitted to the hospital. John was feeling like he wanted to harm himself. He had already taken the cap of a pen and cut his arms with it.

He was admitted to the children's psychiatric unit. They wanted to observe him and get his meds under control. Apparently the ones he was taking were not working. He had some episodes while in this unit; he flipped his bed and pulled the curtains off the wall. He was placed in a padded room and was finally moved downstairs to the adult ward. They did not want him around the other kids. He apparently got in trouble for trying to comfort a girl his age by hugging her, and they have no-touch rules. Again, his anger took over.

John's dad blamed himself for John's breakdown and he told John that he would be there for him from now on. Yeah, right.

John was kept in the hospital until they felt he was stable enough and his meds were working. He was not to return to his regular school yet, so he went to a day treatment center where they could continue to monitor his meds, and he could have tutors help him to keep up with his school work. John is really an intelligent person. He did well with his classes, and then he went back to his school for the last three weeks of school. He passed the 10th grade.

He seemed to be doing better until school started again. Then the trouble started all over again, only this time there was more trouble than he could handle. One of the visits that John made to his father's house, he was on the computer while his father was out mowing the woods. He found some porn on his dad's computer. It was all sorts of pictures of women getting spanked. Well, now John's mind went into overdrive, and when he saw a photo where the girl looked almost exactly like one of his sisters, he flipped out. He called his sister and asked her to come up to his father's house and pick him up.

Then when she got him home, he whipped out the picture and she started to cry. Now they knew that the real reason that they got spanked. John felt guilty for what his father had done to his sisters; and John also had to deal with the thought that when he was the one being spanked, was it for the same reason? Then when their mother came home from work, she had the horrid task of facing her worst nightmare. She wanted to kill her ex-husband for what he had done to her children. She confronted him, and she told him how badly she wanted to beat him to death.

Then she went to John's room there and took everything that that belonged to him and told his father to never call or come near them again. If John wanted to have a relationship with him, John would call *him*. The girls were in their 20s now, but this new knowledge still had a terrible effect on them.

John's father went into serious counseling to help him with his alcohol addiction and the other things. After telling John that he was going to be there for him from now on, not only did he cause so much heartache for all, but he also married a woman who lived 40 miles away. He sold the house and moved up her way.

John did not have much to do with his father for a long time after that. He still had a lot of anger inside, and he still had school avoidance issues. In fact, he walked out of school the middle of his junior year. He refused to go back. The guidance counselor told him that he only needed 3 classes to graduate. So with his psychological issues, John was accepted into the alternative education program where the students work on their own to read the text books and take tests to pass the courses. John took senior English, Psychology, and Earth Science and passed all three courses with high A's and graduated from high school 1 year early—a month after he turned 17.

He did not want to go to college, and he wasn't old enough to work adult jobs yet, so he worked in a restaurant grilling steaks and working the line. That was okay for a while, but he soon got bored with it, so he got involved in the car industry. He started out as auto recon, cleaning up cars, then he moved to the parts department, the service department, and now he is manager of the service department for a huge auto conglomerate.

His step-mother works there in the office, so he sees her every day. They have a good relationship. He has also forgiven his father for all of the atrocities that John and his sisters endured at his hand. When everything was uncovered, he went into intensive therapy. He has since apologized to the twins and his son and John and he are working at having a relationship as adults.

John married his high school sweetheart right before he turned 21, and they now have three children. He is a wonderful husband to his wife, and above all, he is an awesome father to his kids. He has two boys and a girl. He adores each one of them. He is 32 and very stable. He works very hard at his job so that his wife can be a stay-at-home mother and together they are awesome parents. John has become the kind of man that any mother would be very proud to have. I know, because I am his mother.

When I look at my son, I see a warm, loving and stable man. I see the little boy that he was, the teenager that I had no idea if he would live to adulthood. It amazes me how he has grown up so well and became a man who is so much more than he ever experienced with the father he had or didn't have. I see a man who learned unconditional love from his mother and his grandparents and his sisters.

I know that little boys really need that father that we all dream of, but we all have to play the hand that we are dealt in life. We have to pull all of the positive things out of life that we can. John has done that. It wasn't easy for him. But he is a man. And as all the others have said in this book:

He is his own man.

Jason's Story

Jason is a 24-year-old man who has a different kind of story to tell than all of the others in this book. Jason is a man who grew up without his father. He was not ignored, pushed away, abused, nor was his father in prison. His father died of brain cancer when Jason was only 5 years old. He has some memories of his father, but not a whole lot of them. His father was ill for a couple years before he died at the age of 42. As if that was not enough, two years after his father died, his mother died of breast cancer at the age of 40.

His mother knew that she was dying, so she moved herself and her two children, Jason and his younger sister back to her hometown. She bought a small home and asked her sister and brother-in-law to live in this house and raise her children after she was gone. So after her death, the aunt and uncle tried to be the parents that these children had lost. They were very religious and very strict, which worked well for the little girl. It didn't work well for Jason.

Jason gave them problems at every turn. When visiting his paternal grandparents, Jason got into a little trouble and his aunt and uncle did not want him to come back. So Jason was separated from his sister and remained living with his grandparents who were in their 70s. Jason was in junior high school.

Now his problems became worse; he went from strict Born Again Christians to 70+ year-old grandparents. His grandfather was extremely strict and grouchy, and his grandmother spoiled him and tried to undo everything that grandpa did. Jason still had problems with school, with friends, with grandparents. He had a lot of anger inside of him for having lost his parents at such a young age, being rejected by his aunt and uncle, and then the confusing signals he got from the grandparents.

Jason could charm the skin off a snake, and then he could turn around and cause more trouble than you can imagine. He became very adept at lying, telling people what they want to hear and manipulating people and the truth to suit his purposes. He quit everything he started: sports, the band, jobs. He moved out of his grandparents' house in his senior year and moved in with one of his friends until they figured out that he was a manipulator.

Upon graduation, he joined the Marine Corps. That lasted for a few months. He hated it; he got hurt, and was discharged. Back home again.

One of his half-sisters took him into her home twice until he caused enough trouble that she had to ask him to leave. His sister's mother—his father's first wife—invited him to stay with her. She tried to help him get into school for something that he thought he would enjoy. That lasted for a semester until he caused trouble at school and then he dropped out. He soon wore out his welcome with her, when he lied about something that was a horrible lie to cover his infidelity with his girlfriend at the time. During this time, grandfather was dying of emphysema and lung cancer.

Jason moved back home with Grandma, but instead of being a help to her, he caused her more problems. He got himself arrested for speeding, DUI, driving without a license and for making terroristic threats. Grandma ended up paying for the school loans because he could not hold down a job, and because he ended up going to jail for all of the things listed above. He spent almost 9 months in jail and lost his license.

He is now living back with Grandma, he is still driving without a license, but at least he has a job. He found that he has a love for cars and he has a job working with auto parts. He just had his 24th birthday. Jason's natural sister doesn't associate with him at all. His older sisters try to be positive role models for him, and they try to include him in family gatherings so he has some semblance of family.

Would things have been a whole lot different with Jason if he had his father while he was growing up? It is hard to tell. He seemed to use the whole "orphan" thing to his advantage, but no one but him really knows how he feels. He was denied having his father in his life, so it is unlikely that he would turn to religion for comfort.

When he was asked to comment on his growing up without his father, Jason said that because he was so young when his father died, it seemed normal to him. But reflecting on it now, he believes that not having his father left some holes in the person he is now—mainly how to deal with relationships and keep them. He feels that he is a difficult person to get along with. He is friendly, but never open. He keeps a lot to himself. He believes that his father might have been abler to help him with that. (But I know that he is very much like his father when he was young.)

Jason says that there is a plus side to everything— he has learned to really appreciate his family more than most. Not having a father has made him old in many ways and younger in others. He says that he is always so serious about things (so was his father and grandfather).

Jason believes that he started to feel the anger of having lost his parents when he was a teenager. But now he has seemed to find some peace in himself, but Christmas is always a dark day for him, as it was on Christmas afternoon that his father passed away. He has come to really appreciate his family—the family that he has left.

He sends a message to the readers of this book. "You are not alone. It might seem like it on your deepest, darkest day, but the reality of It is that you are never alone. Stand your ground, fight your fears and know that you don't have to go it alone. There are people who will hold your hand and fight with you."

This is a young man struggling to be his own man.

Part Three
The Products of Fatherless Homes

Statistics of Fatherless Sons

There have been many studies done about fatherless sons and their lots in life. Statistics are astounding. It seems that 63% of youth suicides are from fatherless homes. And 90% of all runaways and homeless kids are from fatherless families. Children with behavior issues consist of 85% fatherless children. Rapists with anger problems, 80% of them were fatherless. And 71% of all high school dropouts come from fatherless homes. It is hard to believe that the numbers are so high. It must mean that there IS a fatherless stigma that affects this generation.

Another statistic shows that 75% of adolescent patients in chemical abuse clinics come from fatherless homes. Columbia University researched and found that even in 2-parent homes where the children have a bad relationship with their fathers, 68% were more apt to smoke, drink alcohol, or use drugs when compared with other kids in 2-parent homes. Teens in single mother households are 30% higher risks than in the 2-parent homes.

Then looking at prisons, 85% of all youths in prison are from fatherless homes. Youths who never had a father in the households experienced the highest odds. And 1/5 of incarcerated youths had a father who had been or was still in jail or prison.

Looking at child abuse and absent fathers, the statistics are also unbelievable. Comparing children in 2-parent and single parent households, the children with only one parent has double the risk factor of suffering physical, emotional or educational neglect.

According to the US Department of Census, 43% of United States children live without a father present in the home. Seventy-one percent of pregnant teenagers come from fatherless homes. Fatherless boys and girls are 2-times as likely to quit school; twice as likely to end up in jail; four times more likely to need professional help for emotional or behavioral issues. (http://www.fathermag.com/news/2778-stats.shtml)

Yes, it sounds quite astounding, doesn't it? But what the surveys cannot measure is whether or not these things would still happen if the loser and dead-beat dads would have been IN the households. When you read some of the stories of the boys/men in this book, you can see ways that having their fathers in their lives caused damage and emotional scars that may never heal. The fact of the matter is that kids do not need **_A_** father; they need a **_GOOD_** father in their lives.

Famous People Who Grew up Without Fathers

There are many famous people who grew up without fathers. This is important to show that many fatherless children can grow up to have their dreams come true. These people went on without their fathers to become successful and some of them are even wealthy!

The following people lost their fathers to death: Kate Beckinsale's father died when she was 6. Orlando Bloom's died when he was 4. Bill Clinton lost his father in a car accident 3 months before he was born. Stephen Colbert lost his father and two brothers in a plane crash when he was 10. Sean Combs was 3 when his father was murdered. Kid Cudi lost his father to cancer when he was 11. Jet Li lost his father when he was 2. Shelby Lynne lost her mother and father in a murder suicide when she was 17. Eddie Murphy's father was killed when he was just 8. President Barack Obama met his father only once before he died in a car crash. Guy Pearce lost his father in a work related accident when he was 8. Julia Roberts lost her father when she was 10. Jason Schwartzman lost his father to cancer when he was 13. Barbra Streisand lost her father when she was 2. Orson Welles lost his mother when he was 11 and his father when he was 15. This list includes 2 U.S. Presidents!!

This next list contains celebrities who were abandoned by their fathers. Notorious B.I.G. was abandoned by his father when he was 2. Halle Berry was abandoned by her father when she was 4. Mary J. Blige was abandoned by her father when she was 4. Pierce Brosnan was abandoned by his father before his first birthday. Jamie Foxx was abandoned by both his parents and raised by his adopted grandparents. Laird Hamilton was abandoned by his father when he was an infant. Jay-Z was abandoned by his father. Demi Moore was abandoned by her father before she was born. Clive Owen was abandoned by his father when he was 3. Keanu Reeves was abandoned by his father when he was 13. Alex Rodriguez was abandoned by his father when he was 7. Gene Simmons was abandoned by his father when he was 3. David Spade was abandoned by his father. Shania Twain was abandoned by her birth father. Kanye West was abandoned by his father when he was 3. It has been going on for some time now. Don't you wonder if their fathers ever came back to see if they could cash in on their sons' or daughters' fortunes? It takes all kinds.

And another group of celebs never knew their fathers or did not even know who they were: Lance Armstrong never knew his birth father. 50 Cent never knew his father and lost his mother when he was 8. Eric Clapton never knew his real father. He grew up thinking his grandparents were his parents and his mother his sister. Adrian Grenier grew up not knowing who his father was. Jack Nicholson never knew his real father. Tupac Shakur grew up not knowing his birth father while his stepfather went to prison when he was 2. Liv Tyler didn't know who her birth father was until she was 9.

And finally, this group lost their fathers through divorce, and some were sent to live with their grandparents—so they lost both parents. But they still had enough self-esteem to get them to where they are to-day—with fame and fortune. Jon Stewart was raised primarily by his mother. Mariah Carey eventually became estranged from her father after her parents' divorce when she was 3. Al Pacino grew up in his grandparents' home with his mother. Shaquille O'Neal grew up without his birth father. Marilyn Monroe grew up without a father. Eva Mendes was raised by her single mother after her parents divorced. Lindsay Lohan grew up without a father while he was in prison. John Lennon grew up without a father and lost his mother when he was 17. Martin Lawrence rarely saw his father after his parents divorced when he was 8. Alicia Keys grew up without a father. Samuel L. Jackson only met his father twice during his life. Jodie Foster grew up without a father; her parents separated before she was born. Maya Angelou was sent to live with her grandparents when her parents' marriage ended. Oprah Winfrey was born to an unwed, teenager mother and sent to live with her grandparents.

(http://us.wow.com/search?sfatherless%20celebrities).

So while there are many people who do not weather the life without a father so well, there are, in contrast, many people who did not let it stand in their way of being their own man or woman. How does this happen? I don't believe that very many people know the answer to that question. The best advice that these celebrities would probably give someone who has grown up in similar situations, would be to follow your dream, become your own person, and do not compare yourself to the missing parent. Don't give another thought to that deadbeat dad who abandoned you for whatever reason. It was NOT about you—I promise! Focus on the people in your life who love and support you; and identify with them, for they are truly the wind beneath your sails.

Conclusion

Power of Forgiveness

Ever since my teenage years, I always wondered why you did what you did. I always wondered why for some reason you didn't put a father figure or male role model in my life. Why I lived in the neighborhood I lived in, why I had to watch my mother struggle, and get abused. I wondered why I was the one that got talked about in middle school, why I was the one afraid to ask my mom for things when I knew she couldn't afford it. Sometimes I wondered why I never had the opportunity to wear name brand shoes.

I finally understand, GOD. It was to teach me how to become a real man. It was to teach me how to stand up for what's right, and to be the man of my household. It was to teach me how to make a way out of no way. I finally understand, GOD. Yes, I get it. For days now, I have been thinking about my whole past, and it just put a big smile on my face. I was really able to see and understand that everything happens for a reason. When one door closes, another one opens. I am just so grateful for everything you have done in my life, and I just want to say thank you. Thank you, for life.

As I come to the end of such a life-learning experience, I just want to thank a few people who have helped me make one of my dreams come true. First, and most important, I want to thank my God. He may not come when you want him to, but He'll be there right on time. He's an on-time God. Yes, He is. Second, I want to thank my mother, family, and friends for the support, criticism, and advice that helped me along the way to insure this book is its best. A very big thanks to my high school teacher, Mr. K, for his outstanding work and motivation. Thank you to everyone who purchased my book. You truly don't understand how you have all affected my life, and I am greatly appreciative. Last, I want to thank my dad. Thank you for working with me as I expressed my feelings. Thank you for working with me to improve our communication; I am happy to have a better relationship with you. The importance of this is to express the Power of Forgiveness! I love you all. Thanks for reading!

"Again Jesus spoke to them, saying, "I am the light of the world. Whoever follows me will not walk in darkness, but will have the light of life."

John 8:12

Young men and ladies, sometimes the best way to help you move forward is to forgive and forget. So, I challenge you to write a personal letter to your mother, father, brother, sister, aunt, uncle, grandmother, or grandfather that you feel failed to be a part of your life. This is your opportunity to vent, and express your feelings to them. No one said anything about showing them; that's your decision. Writing and talking about your feelings is a fresh way to start forgiving and forgetting.

We can all be our own men!

Afterword

I wanted to add an afterthought to my book. As I have Sickle Cell Disease, I want to give some information that may also be helpful to others.

Pain, pain, and more pain is all I felt growing up with a life changing disease. Sickle Cell disease is a blood disorder where red blood cells are sickle shaped instead of normal or circular shaped. Sickle cell, from my understanding, affects African Americans, Hispanics, and others. There are a few different types of sickle cell. I would consider them to be normal, mild, and severe.

Many patients suffering from sickle cell anemia are at the severe stage. Sickle Cell pain affects every patient differently. In my family, I wasn't the only child growing up and having to deal with this disease. My sister Ciara and my Cousin Jessica also were diagnosed. Now, what I meant about sickle cell affecting us all differently is that for my sister, her pain was primarily in her stomach, back, and legs. My pain, the majority of the time, would be in my legs and arms. My cousin, on the other hand, her pain would be throughout her entire body. I was diagnosed with sickle cell disease at two weeks old, and from that day and on, my health has been a continuous challenge.

Separate from living in a father-absent home, my childhood was filled with many visits to the children's emergency room. Going to the emergency room often became like a weekly routine. My mom stated that while in extreme amounts of pain, I would sometimes crawl on the floor because I didn't want to put any pressure on my legs. To be honest, I couldn't. One word to describe my pain would be, horrible. I'm often asked the question of what sickle cell pain really feels like. Some even ask me about the life expectancy of patients living with Sickle Cell. My sickle cell pain, to use my legs as an example, feels like sharp pain that becomes a rhythm with my heart beat. Every time my heart beats, that's exactly when I get a sharp pain in my legs or even arms. So imagine what that feels like.

My sickle cell pain didn't just last for a few minutes, but the majority of the time it lasted a week, sometimes two. It was always hospital after hospital, but this was my life. I can't sit here and tell you all that I accepted the fact that I was a young kid diagnosed with sickle cell that basically took over my whole childhood. I can't sit here and tell you all that I didn't blame God or life in general for such hard obstacles. If I was to sit here and tell you that I didn't, that would be a lie. I did. Each and every day, I questioned my faith in God. I questioned my purpose in life. I even sometimes questioned why I was here on earth, knowing that every day for the rest of my life I would be in pain, living with a life changing disease. I hated sickle cell. I hated the person that sickle cell turned me into at that time. Being in extreme amounts of pain on most occasions, I turned into something I knew for a fact I wasn't. I didn't want to be bothered with anyone, not even my own family. I sometimes would have the biggest attitude towards people.

I couldn't accept the fact that I was five, six, seven, and eight and so on years old, not being able to go swimming or enjoy any physical activities. I found my-self sitting on the side lines watching while most of my neighborhood friends enjoyed themselves. My mom would always try to protect me and keep me from hav-ing pain in my body, but sometimes I just had to go for it.

I remember one evening in the hot summer time, all of the neighborhood kids and adults were all headed down to the community pool. I already knew from past experiences that getting in the cold water, especially an outdoor pool, would cramp up my legs. Do I want to go back through the emergency again? Did I want to be in pain for the next two weeks, and not be able to go to school or even play outside? I kept asking myself these questions over and over again, because I didn't know exactly what to do. What would I do while everyone was down in the swimming pool having fun? Would I enjoy myself sitting there watching everyone?

At this point I was so confused. I told my mom that I was going outside to see what everyone was do-ing, knowing that I already knew. For some reason my mom knew what I was up to. She told me that I bet not be thinking about going down the street to get in the pool. That's not going to happen! I tried to lie to her and tell her I wasn't, but she already was two steps ahead of me. I was surprised when she told me I could go down the street, but I couldn't come back and ask her if I could get in. I walked out the door and headed down the street.

Everyone was running past me in shorts and with their beach towels. Come on God! I felt like I was being tested, because I loved water, but knew what it would do to me. I knew my mom would be upset with me if I tried to get in without her permission. I know my mom very well. She is the type of mother that would come down the street just to see if you followed her directions. Where our house was, one could stand on the front porch and look all the way down to the park. I knew if she didn't see me sitting there, then she would rush down to see where I was. I finally made it down to the pool area next to the park, and saw everyone having the time of their lives. I wanted to get some of that action myself, but there was no way I would get away with it. Hmmm.... Could I sneak back in the house and change my clothes without my mother seeing me; and then will I be able to take a dip in the cool water? How would I sneak back in the house?

My sister was down in the pool too and I knew she would run and tell. I bet she would love to see me get in trouble and witness yet another whooping. I'm doing it, I have to. I began running back down to my house and one of my neighbors was walking down to the pool. She asked me what I was doing, and why I wasn't down in the pool having fun. I told her that I was on my way into my house to change my clothes, and asked her to wait for me. I wanted to trick my sister into believing that mom allowed me to get my feet wet with supervision. I opened the door quietly, and listened for my mom. It was complete silence for a split second, but then there was laughter. Ha! I got her.

She was upstairs on the phone with someone having, I guess, a good conversation. I couldn't tell if her door was closed or open. I knew if I was going to get in the pool I had to change my clothes, but that would require me to go past her room. People didn't believe me when I said that my mom had eyes behind her head. Her room was set up perfectly. She often sat on her bed facing the opposite direction of her room door watching television. Next to her TV was a mirror that saw everything behind her. Our stairs always made noise while walking on them, so I just knew I would be caught. She started laughing louder and I knew this would be my only opportunity. So I went for it, and ran past her door and into my room. I hurried and changed my clothes, but covered myself in regular clothing to try to trick my mother. I made it all the way back down stairs without her seeing what I was up to.

I continued to run down into our basement to change my clothes for the second time. I couldn't believe what I was doing, but I knew what the consequences were. Not only would I be in pain, but I would be on punishment for days. Nope that didn't change my mindset either. My mind was made up and to the pool, here I come. I walked outside and met up with my neighbor and walked down to the pool once again. We showed our pass to get in; and from there, I was free. I couldn't believe for the first time I was actually on the other side of the gate. My sister saw me and asked what I was doing in there.

"Mom said I can come," I replied. I knew exactly what I was going to do, take a big dip in this nice looking water before my mom came down here and caught me. I did just that. I stayed in the water for about an hour, and immediately felt sick. I got out as fast as I could and lay down in the hot sun, but it was too late. The pain hit me in an instance, and I just started walking home. I knew I shouldn't have gotten in that water, but I couldn't resist it. Man! My mom is going to be so mad at me for disobeying her authority. I'm sorry God. I just wanted to feel free, and not being able to do what my friends were doing made me feel trapped. I made it back to my house and walked in the door.

My mom was standing in the kitchen and started yelling. I told you not to get in that water! I started crying not because of her yelling at me, but because I could barely stand due to the sharp pain rising through my right leg. I went and lay in my bed, and my mom came and took care of me. She knew I always wanted to do what my friends were doing, but I just couldn't. The next few days my pain went away, and from that day on, I promised myself and God that I would never disobey my mother or get back in a swimming pool. I must say that I did try again years later, and I am proud to say that I was pain free! Since growing up, my sickle cell has calmed down a little bit.

Compared to my early childhood, my visits to the emergency room have changed from weekly to yearly. I often thank God for giving me the strength to battle this disease every day. I must admit that even though my sickle cell has calmed, I still to this day face many challenges. No longer do I blame God or anyone else for sickle cell; I smile now when I talk about it because it has changed my life. Sickle Cell has contributed to much of my success today.

Due to me not being able to play physical activities, I turned to leadership and business. Due to my Sickle Cell, I can proudly announce that I am a 21 year old CEO of my own corporation in the State of Michigan. Yes God!

This book is dedicated to my beautiful single mother,
Ursula Hardy.

CPSIA information can be obtained at www.ICGtesting.com
Printed in the USA
LVOW11s1105250215

428317LV00001B/10/P

9 780578 140537